GW00706164

Exley Publications Ltd,
16 Chalk Hill, Watford, Herts WD19 4BG, United Kingdom.
Exley Publications LLC, 185 Main Street, Spencer, MA 01562, USA.
www.helenexleygiftbooks.com

Copyright © Helen Exley 1992, 2003
**Series editor: Helen Exley**
The moral right of the author has been asserted.
First published in 1992, revised 2003

Published simultaneously in the USA by Exley Publications LLC and
in Great Britain by Exley Publications Ltd, 2003

12 11 10 9 8 7 6 5 4 3 2 1

ISBN 1-86187-534-7

A copy of the CIP data is available from the British Library on request.

Edited by Helen Exley.
Pictures researched by Image Select International.
Designed by 451°. Printed in China.

Exley Publications is very grateful to the following individuals and
organizations for permission to reproduce their pictures:
Archiv Für Kunst: 29; Austrian Institute, London: 59; Bettman Archive: 10;
Bridgeman Art Library: 12, 14, 16/17, 21, 23, 39, 43, Dora Holzhandler,
"Lovers in Holland Park" © 2003, 51, 61; Brooklyn Museum New York: 39,
Marc Chagall "Fiances on a Green Background" © DACS 1991, 43,
"La Passagiata" © DACS 1991, 53; Christies Colour Library: 6/7, 30/31, 35,
John Waterhouse, "The Awakening of Adonis", cover, title-page and 56;
Mary Evans Picture Library: 19; Fine Art Photographic Library; Giraudon: 8,
25, 49, 54; Guildhall Art Gallery: 16/17, 23; Hermitage Museum: 47;
Image Select: 59; Jerzy Marek "A Room with a View", 37; Musee d'Orsay: 49;
Museum der Stadt, Vienna: 29; Narodni Gallery Prague: 14, Pablo Picasso
"L'appuntamento" © DACS 1991, 41; Scala: 26, 41, 53; Tate Picture Library:
E.Burne-Jones, "Clerk Saunders", 45; Victoria and Albert Museum: 61.

# Words on being madly in Love

*Words* *on being madly in*

# Love

A HELEN EXLEY GIFTBOOK

WHOSO LOVES... BELIEVES THE IMPOSSIBLE.

*elizabeth barrett browning* (1806-1861)

THERE IS NO REMEDY FOR LOVE BUT TO LOVE MORE.

*henry david thoreau* (1817 - 1862)

EXPERIENCE SEEMS TO CONVINCE US THAT ONLY
FOOLS TRUST, THAT ONLY FOOLS BELIEVE AND ACCEPT
ALL THINGS. IF THIS IS TRUE, THEN LOVE IS MOST
FOOLISH, FOR IF IT IS NOT FOUNDED ON TRUST,
BELIEF AND ACCEPTANCE, IT'S NOT LOVE.

*leo buscaglia*

LOVE IS THE TRIUMPH OF IMAGINATION OVER INTELLIGENCE.

*h. l. mencken* (1880 - 1956)


IF THOU REMEMBER'ST NOT THE SLIGHTEST FOLLY
THAT EVER LOVE DID MAKE THEE RUN INTO,
THOU HAST NOT LOVED.

*william shakespeare* (1564 - 1616)
*from "As You Like It"*


LOVE WORKS MIRACLES EVERY DAY: SUCH AS WEAKENING
THE STRONG, AND STRENGTHENING THE WEAK; MAKING
FOOLS OF THE WISE, AND WISE MEN OF FOOLS; FAVOURING
THE PASSIONS, DESTROYING REASON, AND, IN A WORD,
TURNING EVERYTHING TOPSY-TURVY.

*marguerite de valois*


LOVE LOOKS NOT WITH THE EYES,
BUT WITH THE MIND;
AND THEREFORE IS WINGED CUPID PAINTED BLIND.

*william shakespeare* (1564 - 1616)
*from "A Midsummer Night's Dream"*

ROMANTIC LOVE "HAPPENS"; IT IS NOT BROUGHT
ABOUT; ONE FALLS IN LOVE. THE PERSON IS
OBSESSED WITH THE LOVED ONE AND IS UNABLE TO
CONCENTRATE ON ANYTHING ELSE. THE PERSON
LOSES ALL DESIRE TO REMAIN INDEPENDENT, AND
INSTEAD DESIRES TO MERGE AND SUBSUME
... INTO THE OTHER.

*margaret horton*


LOVE IS LIKE FEVER; IT COMES AND GOES WITHOUT
THE WILL HAVING ANY PART IN THE PROCESS.

*henry beyle stendahl* (1783 - 1842)


O LYRIC LOVE, HALF ANGEL AND HALF BIRD
AND ALL A WONDER AND A WILD DESIRE.

*robert browning* (1812 - 1889)

LOVE MUST BE LEARNED, AND LEARNED AGAIN;
THERE IS NO END TO IT.

*katherine anne porter* (1890 - 1980)


PERFECT LOVE IS RARE INDEED... TO BE A LOVER
WILL REQUIRE THAT YOU CONTINUALLY HAVE THE
SUBTLETY OF THE VERY WISE, THE FLEXIBILITY OF
THE CHILD, THE SENSITIVITY OF THE ARTIST,
THE UNDERSTANDING OF THE PHILOSOPHER, THE
ACCEPTANCE OF THE SAINT, THE TOLERANCE OF THE
SCHOLAR, AND THE FORTITUDE OF THE CERTAIN.

*leo buscaglia*


THERE IS ALWAYS SOMETHING LEFT TO LOVE.
AND IF YOU AIN'T LEARNED THAT, YOU AIN'T
LEARNED NOTHING.

*lorraine hansberry* (1930 - 1965)

LOVE AND JOY ARE TWINS,

OR BORN OF EACH OTHER.

*william hazlitt* (1778 - 1830)


O FAIR! O SWEET! WHEN I DO LOOK ON THEE,

IN WHOM ALL JOYS SO WELL AGREE,

HEART AND SING IN ME,

JUST ACCORD ALL MUSIC MAKE.

*richard sheridan* (1751 - 1816)


THE BEST AND MOST BEAUTIFUL THINGS IN THE

WORLD CANNOT BE SEEN OR EVEN TOUCHED.

THEY MUST BE FELT WITH THE HEART.

*helen keller* (1880 - 1968)


LOVE DOESN'T MAKE THE WORLD GO ROUND.

LOVE IS WHAT MAKES THE RIDE WORTHWHILE.

*franklin p. jones*

YOU CAN REMEMBER THE SECOND AND THE THIRD
AND THE FOURTH TIME, BUT THERE'S NO TIME LIKE
THE FIRST. IT'S ALWAYS THERE.

*shelagh delaney, b.* 1939


THE MAGIC OF FIRST LOVE IS OUR IGNORANCE
THAT IT CAN EVER END.

*benjamin disraeli* (1804 - 1881)

LOVE IS THE IRRESISTIBLE DESIRE TO BE
DESIRED IRRESISTIBLY.

*louis ginsberg*

LOVE CONSISTS IN THIS, THAT TWO SOLITUDES
PROTECT AND BORDER AND SALUTE EACH OTHER.

*rainer maria rilke* (1875 - 1926)
*from "Letters to a Young Poet"*

LIFE HAS TAUGHT US THAT LOVE DOES NOT CONSIST
IN GAZING AT EACH OTHER, BUT IN LOOKING
OUTWARDS TOGETHER IN THE SAME DIRECTION.

*antoine de saint-exupery* (1900 - 1944)
*from "Airman's Odyssey"*

LOVE IS AN EGOTISM OF TWO.

*antoine de salle*

LOVE IS A GAME THAT TWO CAN PLAY
AND BOTH WIN.

*eva gabor*

LOVE IS BUT THE DISCOVERY OF OURSELVES IN
OTHERS, AND THE DELIGHT IN THE RECOGNITION.

*alexander smith* (1830 - 1867)
*from "Dreamthorp"*

LOVE IS LIFE... AND IF YOU MISS LOVE,
YOU MISS LIFE.

*leo buscaglia*

LOVE IS SPONTANEOUS AND CRAVES EXPRESSION
THROUGH JOY, THROUGH BEAUTY, THROUGH TRUTH,
EVEN THROUGH TEARS. LOVE LIVES THE MOMENT;
IT'S NEITHER LOST IN YESTERYEAR NOR DOES IT CRAVE
FOR TOMORROW. LOVE IS NOW!

*leo buscaglia*

BUT TO LOVE IS QUITE ANOTHER THING: IT IS TO WILL
AN OBJECT FOR ITSELF, TO REJOICE IN ITS BEAUTY AND
GOODNESS FOR THEMSELVES, AND WITHOUT RESPECT
TO ANYTHING OTHER THAN ITSELF.

*etienne gilson* (1884 - 1978)
*from The Gifford Lectures*

LOVE COMMANDS US TO STEP OUT INTO
NOTHINGNESS — AND BEARS US UP.

*pam brown, b.*1928

# *love's reward*

YOU MAY BE DECEIVED IF YOU TRUST TOO MUCH, BUT YOU
WILL LIVE IN TORMENT IF YOU DO NOT TRUST ENOUGH.

*frank crane*

IF THOU MUST LOVE ME, LET IT BE FOR NAUGHT
EXCEPT FOR LOVE'S SAKE ONLY.

*elizabeth barrett browning* (1806 - 1861)

LOVE IS LOVE'S REWARD.

*john dryden* (1631 - 1700)

ANY TIME THAT IS NOT SPENT ON LOVE IS WASTED.

*tasso* (1544 - 1595)

PHOEBE: GOOD SHEPHERD, TELL THIS
YOUTH WHAT 'TIS TO LOVE.
SILVUS: IT IS TO BE ALL MADE OF SIGHS AND TEARS…
IT IS TO BE ALL MADE OF FAITH AND SERVICE…
IT IS TO BE ALL MADE OF FANTASY
ALL MADE OF PASSION, AND ALL MADE OF WISHES;
ALL ADORATION, DUTY AND OBSERVANCE;
ALL HUMBLENESS, ALL PATIENCE,
AND IMPATIENCE;
ALL PURITY, ALL TRIAL, ALL OBEISANCE.

*william shakespeare* (1564 - 1616)
*from "As You Like It"*


IT IS LOVE, AND NOT GERMAN PHILOSOPHY, THAT IS
THE TRUE EXPLANATION OF THIS WORLD, WHATEVER
MAY BE THE EXPLANATION OF THE NEXT.

*oscar wilde* (1854 - 1900)

Love seeketh not itself to please,
Nor for itself hath any care,
But for another gives its ease,
And builds a Heaven in Hell's despair.

*william blake* (1757 - 1827)


Life's short and we never have enough
time for the hearts of those who travel
the way with us. O, be swift to love!
Make haste to be kind.

*henri-frederick amiel* (1821 - 1881)


The best portion of a good man's life:
his little nameless, unremembered acts
of kindness and of love.

*william wordsworth* (1770 - 1850)

LOVE IS NOT "BLIND" BUT VISIONARY: IT SEES
INTO THE VERY HEART OF ITS OBJECT, AND SEES THE
"REAL SELF" BEHIND AND IN THE MIDST OF THE
FRAILTIES AND SHORTCOMINGS OF THE PERSON.

*andras angyal*

BUT LOVE… ADDS A PRECIOUS SEEING TO THE EYE;
A LOVER'S EYES WILL GAZE AN EAGLE BLIND;
A LOVER'S EARS WILL HEAR THE LOWEST SOUND,
WHEN THE SUSPICIOUS HEAD OF THEFT IS STOPP'D:
LOVE'S FEELING IS MORE SOFT AND SENSIBLE
THAN ARE THE TENDER HORNS OF COCKLED SNAILS.

*william shakespeare* (1564 - 1616)
*from "Love's Labour's Lost"*

AS SELFISHNESS AND COMPLAINT PERVERT AND
CLOUD THE MIND, SO LOVE WITH ITS JOYS CLEARS
AND SHARPENS THE VISION.

*helen keller* (1880 - 1968)

You've been in love; you know what it's like. It's a sense of delight, not just in the person you love, but in all people, in yourself, in life. Suddenly you see beauty, excitement everywhere. You're not afraid to express your love: passionately, gently, in words, or in silence. And you feel strong, generous, fully alive.

*george weinberg*

LOVE IS A FEELING THAT EMANATES FROM
THE HEART AND EXTENDS THROUGH THE BLOOD
TO EVERY CELL OF THE BODY.

*alexander lowen*

WE ARE ALL BORN FOR LOVE. IT IS THE PRINCIPLE
OF EXISTENCE, AND ITS ONLY END.

*benjamin disraeli* (1804 - 1881)

...AND WE OURSELVES SHALL BE LOVED FOR A WHILE
AND FORGOTTEN. BUT THE LOVE WILL HAVE BEEN
ENOUGH; ALL THOSE IMPULSES OF LOVE RETURN TO
THE LOVE THAT MADE THEM. EVEN MEMORY IS NOT
NECESSARY FOR LOVE. THERE IS A LAND OF THE
LIVING AND A LAND OF THE DEAD, AND THE BRIDGE IS
LOVE, THE ONLY SURVIVAL, THE ONLY MEANING.

*thornton wilder* (1897 - 1976)

IN THE SILENCE OF NIGHT I HAVE OFTEN WISHED FOR JUST A FEW WORDS OF LOVE FROM ONE MAN, RATHER THAN THE APPLAUSE OF THOUSANDS OF PEOPLE.

*judy garland* (1922 - 1969)

HAVING SOMEONE WONDER WHERE YOU ARE WHEN YOU DON'T COME HOME AT NIGHT IS A VERY OLD HUMAN NEED.

*margaret mead* (1901 - 1978)

LOVE IS THE ONLY THING THAT HOLDS THE DARK AT BAY.

*pam brown, b.*1928

ONE WORD

FREES US OF ALL THE WEIGHT AND PAIN OF LIFE:

THAT WORD IS LOVE.

*sophocles* (496 - 405 *b.c.*)

THOSE WHO LOVE DEEPLY NEVER GROW OLD;
THEY MAY DIE OF OLD AGE, BUT THEY DIE YOUNG.

*sir arthur wing pinero* (1855 - 1934)


LOVE, ALL ALIKE, NO SEASON KNOWS, NOR CLIME,
NOR HOURS, DAYS, MONTHS, WHICH ARE THE RAGS OF TIME.

*john donne* (1573 - 1631)


TIME IS
TOO SLOW FOR THOSE WHO WAIT,
TOO SWIFT FOR THOSE WHO FEAR,
TOO LONG FOR THOSE WHO GRIEVE;
TOO SHORT FOR THOSE WHO REJOICE;
BUT FOR THOSE WHO LOVE,
TIME IS ETERNITY.

*henry van dyke* (1852 - 1933)

Love is like quicksilver in the hand.
Leave the fingers open and it stays.
Clutch it, and it darts away.

*dorothy parker* (1893 - 1967)


...Love is always open arms. With arms open you allow love to come and go as it wills, freely, for it'll do so anyway. If you close your arms about love you'll find you are left only holding yourself.

*leo buscaglia*


Him that I love, I wish to be Free – Even from me.

*anne morrow lindbergh* (1906 - 2001)

LOVE IS GREATER THAN ILLUSION, AND AS
STRONG AS DEATH.

*alberto casella*
from "Death Takes A Holiday"


'TIS LOVE THAT MAKES ME BOLD AND RESOLUTE,
LOVE THAT CAN FIND A WAY WHERE PATH THERE'S NONE,
OF ALL THE GODS THE MOST INVINCIBLE.

*euripides* (480 - 406 *b.c.*)
from "Hippolytus"


SET ME AS A SEAL UPON THINE HEART, AS A SEAL
UPON THINE ARM; FOR LOVE IS STRONG AS DEATH;
JEALOUSY IS CRUEL AS THE GRAVE; THE COALS
THEREOF ARE COALS OF FIRE, WHICH HATH A MOST
VEHEMENT FLAME. MANY WATERS CANNOT QUENCH
LOVE, NEITHER CAN THE FLOODS DROWN IT.

*solomon's song*

LOVE FROM ONE BEING TO ANOTHER CAN ONLY
BE THAT TWO SOLITUDES COME NEARER, RECOGNIZE
AND PROTECT AND COMFORT EACH OTHER.

*han suyin*

FOR LOVE IS BUT THE HEART'S IMMORTAL THIRST
TO BE COMPLETELY KNOWN AND ALL FORGIVEN.

*henry van dyke* (1852-1933)
*from "Collected Poems"*

LOVE IS TO UNDERSTAND, AT LAST, THE
SUFFERING OF ANOTHER.

*pam brown, b.*1928

SO OFTEN WHEN WE SAY "I LOVE YOU" WE
SAY IT WITH A HUGE "I" AND A SMALL "YOU".

*anthony bloom*
*Russian Orthodox Archbishop of England*

THE GAME THAT IS SUBJECT TO THE GREATEST
PENALTIES IS LOVE.

*o. a. battista*

EVEN AS LOVE CROWNS YOU SHALL HE CRUCIFY YOU.
EVEN AS HE IS FOR YOUR GROWTH SO IS HE
FOR YOUR PRUNING.

*kahlil gibran* (1883 - 1931)

LOVE IS THE SICKNESS IN WHICH RECOVERY IS LOSS.

*pam brown, b.*1928

ONE MAKES MISTAKES, THAT IS LIFE. BUT IT IS
NEVER QUITE A MISTAKE TO HAVE LOVED.

*romain rolland* (1866 - 1944)
*from "Summer"*

IN THE ARITHMETIC OF LOVE,
ONE PLUS ONE EQUALS EVERYTHING AND
TWO MINUS ONE EQUALS NOTHING.

*mignon mclaughlin*

TAKE LOVE WHEN LOVE IS GIVEN,
BUT NEVER THINK TO FIND IT
A SURE ESCAPE FROM SORROW
OR A COMPLETE REPOSE.

*sara teasdale* (1884 - 1933)
*in "Day's Ending"*

LOVE IS A SPRINGTIME PLANT THAT PERFUMES
EVERYTHING WITH ITS HOPE,
EVEN THE RUINS TO WHICH IT CLINGS.

*gustave flaubert* (1821 - 1880)

LOVE IS LIFE'S END (AN END, BUT NEVER ENDING)

ALL JOYS, ALL SWEETS, ALL HAPPINESS AWARDING;

LOVE IS LIFE'S WEALTH

(NE'ER SPENT, BUT EVER SPENDING),

MORE RICH BY GIVING, TAKING BY DISCARDING;

LOVE'S LIFE'S REWARD, REWARDED IN REWARDING:

THEN FROM THY WRETCHED HEART

FOND CARE REMOVE;

AH, SHOULD THOU LIVE BUT ONCE

LOVE'S SWEETS TO PROVE,

THOU WILT NOT LOVE TO LIVE UNLESS

THOU LIVE TO LOVE.

*author unknown*
from "Brittain's Ida", 1628

## the answer

LOVE IS THE ONLY SATISFACTORY ANSWER TO THE

PROBLEM OF HUMAN EXISTENCE.

*erich fromm* (1900 - 1980)

LOVE IS THE MAGICIAN, THE ENCHANTER, THAT
CHANGES WORTHLESS THINGS TO JOY, AND MAKES
RIGHT-ROYAL KINGS AND QUEENS OF COMMON CLAY.
IT IS THE PERFUME OF THAT WONDROUS FLOWER, THE
HEART, AND WITHOUT THAT SACRED PASSION, THAT
DIVINE SWOON, WE ARE LESS THAN BEASTS: BUT
WITH IT, EARTH IS HEAVEN AND WE ARE GODS.

*r. g. ingersoll* (1833 - 1899)

LOVING CAN MAKE PLAIN PEOPLE BEAUTIFUL.

*linda clark*

LOVE MAKES A SUBTLE MAN OUT OF A CRUDE ONE,
IT GIVES ELOQUENCE TO THE MUTE, IT GIVES
COURAGE TO THE COWARDLY AND MAKES THE IDLE
QUICK AND SHARP.

*juan ruiz*
*from "El Amor"*

WHEN LOVE IS NOT MADNESS, IT IS NOT LOVE.

*pedro calderon de la barca*
*from "El mayor monstruo los celos"*

WHY DID SHE LOVE HIM? CURIOUS FOOL — BE STILL —
IS HUMAN LOVE THE GROWTH OF HUMAN WILL?

*lord byron* (1788 - 1824)

TRY TO REASON ABOUT LOVE AND YOU WILL
LOSE YOUR REASON.

*french proverb*

LOVE IS A GRAVE MENTAL DISEASE.

*plato* (427 - 347 *b.c.*)

IT IS OVERDOING THE THING TO DIE OF LOVE.

*french proverb*

AGE DOES NOT PROTECT YOU FROM LOVE.
BUT LOVE, TO SOME EXTENT, PROTECTS YOU FROM AGE.

*jeanne moreau, b.*1929


THE GRATIFICATION OF THE SENSES SOON BECOMES
A VERY SMALL PART OF THAT PROFOUND AND
COMPLICATED SENTIMENT WHICH WE CALL LOVE.
LOVE, ON THE CONTRARY, IS A UNIVERSAL THIRST FOR
A COMMUNION, NOT MERELY OF THE SENSES, BUT OF
OUR WHOLE NATURE, INTELLECTUAL, IMAGINATIVE
AND SENSITIVE. HE WHO FINDS HIS ANTITYPE,
ENJOYS A LOVE PERFECT AND ENDURING; TIME
CANNOT CHANGE IT, DISTANCE CANNOT REMOVE IT;
THE SYMPATHY IS COMPLETE.

*benjamin disraeli* (1804 - 1881)
*from "Henrietta Temple"*

LOVE IS, ABOVE ALL, THE GIFT OF ONESELF.

*jean anouilh* (1910 - 1987)


THE PLEASURE OF LOVE IS IN LOVING, AND ONE IS
HAPPIER IN THE PASSION ONE FEELS THAN IN THE
PASSION ONE AROUSES IN ANOTHER.

*duc de la rochefoucauld* (1613 - 1680)


THE LOVE WE GIVE AWAY IS THE ONLY
LOVE WE KEEP.

*elbert hubbard* (1856 - 1915)
*from "The Notebook"*


THE STORY OF A LOVE IS NOT IMPORTANT — WHAT IS
IMPORTANT IS THAT ONE IS CAPABLE OF LOVE.

*helen hayes* (1900 - 1993)

YOUTH'S FOR AN HOUR

BEAUTY'S A FLOWER

BUT LOVE IS THE JEWEL THAT WINS THE WORLD.

*moira o'neill*
*from "Songs of the Glens of Antrim"*


LOVE, AS TOLD BY THE SEERS OF OLD,

COMES AS A BUTTERFLY TIPPED WITH GOLD.

FLUTTERS AND FLIES IN SUNLIT SKIES,

WEAVING ROUND HEARTS THAT WERE

ONE TIME COLD.

*algernon charles swinburne* (1837 - 1909)


'TIS THAT DELIGHTSOME TRANSPORT WE CAN FEEL

WHICH PAINTERS CANNOT PAINT,

NOR WORDS REVEAL,

NOR ANY ART WE KNOW OF CAN CONCEAL.

*thomas paine* (1737 - 1809)

I HAVE LEARNED NOT TO WORRY ABOUT LOVE; BUT
TO HONOUR ITS COMING WITH ALL MY HEART.

*alice walker, b.* 1944

LOVE HAS NO OTHER DESIRE BUT TO FULFIL ITSELF.
TO MELT AND BE LIKE A RUNNING BROOK THAT SINGS
ITS MELODY TO THE NIGHT. TO WAKE AT DAWN WITH A
WINGED HEART AND GIVE THANKS FOR ANOTHER
DAY OF LOVING.

*kahlil gibran* (1883 - 1931)

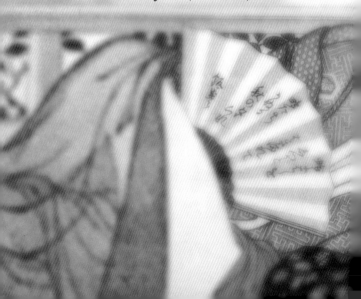

TWO THINGS CANNOT ALTER,
SINCE TIME WAS, NOR TODAY:
THE FLOWING OF WATER;
AND LOVE'S STRANGE, SWEET WAY.

*japanese lyric*